THE COLLEGE GOLF ALMANAC

Brendan M Ryan
Estefania Acosta A.

ISBN: 1548887811
ISBN 13: 9781548887810

Thank you for purchasing the college golf almanac. The book contains empirical data based on the history of college signees on National Junior Golf Scoreboard with data collect at various levels, from NCAA Division I to NJCAA. We hope this information will act as a helpful tool for junior golfers, their families and coaches in understanding where a player might fit within the spectrum of college golf.

The book also contains some basic information for players and their families about the process. This information is a result of years of coaching and thousands of hours visiting schools, speaking to juniors and thinking about the process.

We hope that this will be a tool which will help you in the process. Should you have any further comments or questions, please feel free to reach out to us at brendan@golfplacementservices.com

THE BASICS OF COLLEGE GOLF SCHOLARSHIPS

The NCAA

The NCAA, or National Collegiate Athletic Association, was established in 1906 and serves as the athletics governing body for more than 1,300 colleges, universities, conferences and organizations. The national office is in Indianapolis, Indiana, but the member colleges and universities develop the rules and guidelines for athletics eligibility and athletics competition for each of the three NCAA divisions. The NCAA is committed to the student-athlete and to governing competition in a fair, safe, inclusive and sportsmanlike manner.

The NCAA membership includes:

- 346 active Division I members;
- 298 active Division II members; and
- 440 active Division III members.

One of the differences among the three divisions is that colleges and universities in Divisions I and II may offer athletic scholarships. Division III colleges and universities do not.

Information about NCAA eligibility can be found on the NCAA website at http://ncaa.org.

Schools that Sponsor Golf
Within the NCAA, there are 808 men's programs and 566 women's programs:

Division 1:	298 Men's and 264 Women's program
Division 2:	224 Men's and 166 Women's programs
Division 3:	286 Men's and 136 Women's programs

What is the NAIA?
The National Association of Intercollegiate Athletics (NAIA) is an independent league of colleges and

universities that offer students an opportunity to engage in sports. The leagues' governing body, like the NCAA, oversees the rules and regulations regarding student-athletes in areas such as scholarship, eligibility, amateurism, travel and much more. Going into the 2016-2017 season, the NAIA has 175 men's golf teams and 163 women's golf teams.

What is the NJCAA?

The National Junior College Athletic Association is the governing body of Junior College or two-year schools (according to Golfstat, 62 men's golf programs; 21 women's golf programs). These schools deserve note in this book because I believe they are very strong options for many families, particularly if you believe your student-athlete needs the following:

- A smaller environment to help build skills academically, athletically, socially and help with overall maturity
- Time to develop (Son or daughter has a young biological age)
- You want to go to a larger university but don't have the offers
- Financces are an issues (these schools typically cost less than $15,000 for everything

Number of Scholarships Available

Special Note – The NCAA defines a full scholarship as tuition, fees, room and board and course related text books.

Shown below are the numbers of scholarships allowed:

Men's Golf
NCAA DI: 4.5
NCAA DII: 3.6
NAIA: 5
NJCAA: 8

Women's Golf
NCAA DI: 6
NCAA DII: 5.4
NAIA: 5
NJCAA: 8

What distinguishes a D1 vs D2 vs D3 school?

D1 schools must have 14 sports
D2 schools must have 10 sports
D3 schools must have 8 Sports

.500 rule

In men's D1 golf teams need to have an overall head to head record above .500 to qualify for post-season play. This rule is currently being considered for D1 women's golf.

Eligibility
In D1 and D3 Golf – 5 years to play 4 years
In D2 Golf - 8 semesters

NLI
The National Letter of Intent is binding financial aid offer between the player and the school. National Letters of Intent can only be offered for D1 and D2 schools with scholarships. They can only be offered 2 times a year. Once early and once late. Early is usually about the second week of November. Late is after April 1 until the first day of school.

First Contact
NCAA D1 - September 1 of your Junior Year of High School
NCAA D2 – June 15th between your sophomore and junior year in high school
NCAA D3 – Any time

What are unofficial and unofficial visit?
Official visits can only happen during your senior year, after the university has begun their classes. An

official visit is when the school pays for part or all the costs associated with the visit

What is Countable vs. Non-countable aid?
Non-countable aid is aid that is available to everyone at the institution.

What are the rules for swing coaches?
Swing Coaches can have unlimited and unrestricted communication with a coach under the NCAA rules

Can Player's receive more than a full scholarship?
Cost of attendance is a full scholarship (tuition, fees, room and board and course related text books) plus a stipend. The stipend is usually about 10% of the total cost.

When can coaches make written offers?
A coach cannot make a written offer to D1 prospect until September 1 of their senior year

The Contact Rule and its impact on you
In the past, we had many examples where coaches would wait, miss on athletes and settle at the last minute. I think now that coaches can recruit early, they are less likely to settle on a senior and more likely to get a junior.

For the junior golfer, if you have not heard from any schools by January to March of your junior year, then it is time to act by starting to make lists and communicating with schools.

Funded vs Non-Funded
Based on direct experience, I would estimate that 50 percent of these men's programs are fully funded and 65 percent of the women's programs are. "Fully funded" is technically defined as having the ability to offer the full amount of scholarship under the NCAA rules.

Many people make their decisions based on the label of the division. I find this to be shortsighted, because the worth of a program has less to do with division and more to do with the commitment of the administration, donors and greater community. For example, the Division 2 powerhouse Nova Southeastern University boasts their own golf course, 27,000 students and the perfect weather of South Florida.

I would therefore recommend that student-athletes look at schools in terms of two pools, funded versus non-funded. Funded programs can be defined as any program that has put a strong financial commitment towards golf.

SO, YOU WANT TO PLAY DIVISION I MEN'S GOLF?

J ust about every client I work for wants the same thing — to play Division I college golf. While I never discourage anyone from pursuing this dream, it is my job to recommend the college that best fits the client from a golf, academic, and social standpoint. So, while it would be nice for all of my clients to play at a DI school, it just simply isn't possible. In many cases I am stuck with the unenviable task of explaining to junior golfers and their parents why they may not be Division I material.

The fact of the matter is that recruits and their families have a tough time understanding how few opportunities actually exist in Division I golf, particularly for men. Only 298 Division I schools have men's golf teams, most of which will take an average of two players per recruiting class. This means that there are approximately ***600 Men's Division I roster spots offered per year.***

Those chances seem slim, but they get even slimmer when you take an international perspective into account. As we learned in the previous chapter, according to the European Golf Association, there are 47,178 male junior golfers in Germany, 47,333 juniors in Sweden, and 8,478 juniors in Denmark. Add almost 150,000 juniors in America and the juniors from the fifteen-plus other countries I left out, and those 596 spots are significantly harder to land than most people realize.

Because of the ever-increasing number of prospective student-athletes, coaches need an efficient means to quickly seek out juniors and evaluate their performance. Enter the **Junior Golf Scoreboard (JGS)** and **World Amateur Golf Ranking (WAGR)**, the most accurate ranking systems for junior golfers around the world. Coaches often use these two systems as a way to quickly examine potential recruits. The JGS and WAGR gather data from junior golf tournaments to provide an objective look at how players perform and where they rank with their fellow competitors.

Junior golfers and their parents should pay attention to these rankings to understand the level of performance they need to play at a DI level. Extensive statistical analysis of the JGS and WAGR rankings of players on the JGS list of 2016 Early Signees could tell you exactly how good you need to be. But nobody wants to do that. It is tedious, daunting, and takes far too much time.

Luckily, I did all of that dirty work for you, looking at signings from November 2016.

So you want to play Division I men's golf? Here's how good you need to be:

Recruits from the Top 25 Schools
I split my analysis into three sections of group data, first analyzing the top 25 schools, then the top 26-100, followed by the top 101-150 schools, the top 151-200 schools, the top 201-250 schools, and the top 251-298 schools. Beginning with the top 25 schools, I used data from Golfstats' Top 25 college teams from the end of the Fall Season. There were **67 players signed**, 58 of whom were from the United States and 11 of whom were international players.

In terms of geography, the most recruits in the United States were either from California (12), Florida (6), and Texas (5). Of the 58 American signees, 33 of these players were recruited in-state, 8 were recruited regionally (schools in states near where they live), and 17 were recruited to non-regional out-of-state schools. The international students were from Denmark (2), Philippines, Australia, Norway, Sweden (2), France, Thailand, Ireland, and South Africa.

As far as statistics go, the **average JGS class ranking was 89.45** and **the average WAGR was 533**. While this may seem cut-and-dry, these averages do not paint a full picture of the players recruited to the top 25 teams. There are some outliers.

For example, there was a vast discrepancy in the rankings of players. Although the player with the lowest JGS class ranking was an Oregon recruit from California with a ranking of 5, the highest ranked player was a UNLV recruit from California with a ranking of 406. Although a Norwegian player who was recruited to Texas had the lowest WAGR rank at 87, the player with the highest WAGR was a Thai player ranked at 2256 who was recruited to San Diego State. This player drastically skewed the data; if we took him out then the average WAGR would be 349.57.

TOP 26-100
The second tier of recruits I studied were from the next 75 best Division I men's golf teams. **139 players were signed**, 113 of whom were from the United States and 26 of whom were from international countries.

Out of the 113 American players, 67 signed to in-state schools, 23 signed to regional schools, and 22 signed to non-regional out-of-state schools. The 26 international players were from Costa Rica, Chile, New Zealand (2), Australia (5), Scotland (2), Malaysia, France, Germany, England (4), Spain, Thailand (2), and Canada (5). One of the Australian signees was also a transfer from a junior college.

The **average JGS Class ranking was 191.36** and **the average WAGR was 858.09**. But again, we see these statistics influenced by outliers. For example, the lowest ranked player on the JGS was a South Florida recruit from Florida who was ranked #1, while the highest JGS ranking was a University of Alabama-Birmingham (UAB) recruit from Alabama with a ranking of 1072. The lowest ranked player in the WAGR is a South Florida recruit from Chile with the #7 rank, while the highest ranked player had a WAGR of 2071 and was a Canadian player recruited to Colorado.

NOTE: The sample size of international students registered with the WAGR was too small and showed too much of a discrepancy to consider for the rest of the teams in this study.

TOP 101-150

70 players were signed to the 50 next best schools. Two of the signees were transfers from junior colleges.

Of the 63 players that were from the United States, 34 went to in-state schools, 18 went to regional schools, and 11 went to non-regional out-of-state schools. The 7 international players were signed from Sweden (2), Canada (2), Japan, Czechoslovakia, and Scotland.

The **average JGS Class ranking was 341.77**. The player with the lowest JGS Class ranking of 21 was a Pennsylvanian player who signed to Kansas. The player with the highest JGS Class ranking of 1176 was a player from Wisconsin who signed in-state to Wisconsin.

Top 151-200

63 players were signed to fourth tier of DI colleges I reviewed. Two Junior College transfers were also signed. Of the 54 United States recruits, 27 signed to in-state schools, 16 signed to regional schools, and 11 signed to non-regional out-of-state schools. There were 9 international signees from Canada (3), France, Philippines, England (2), the Dominican Republic, and Japan

The **average JGS Class ranking was 482.98.** The player with the lowest JGS ranking was an Oral Roberts recruit from Oklahoma with a ranking of 41. The player with the highest JGS Class ranking was an Army recruit from North Carolina with a ranking of 1585.

Top 201-250

47 players were signed to the top 201-250 Division 1 men's teams. Of the 43 United States recruits, 19 signed to in-state schools, 14 signed to regional schools, and 10 signed to non-regional out-of-state schools. The 4 international students were from Canada (2), Thailand, and Spain.

The average JGS Class ranking was 516.70. The lowest ranked player was a Rutgers recruit from Maryland with a ranking of 132. The highest ranked player was a Temple recruit from Maryland with a ranking of 1547.

Top 251-298

Only 19 of the final 47 Division I men's golf schools even had Early Signings to report. **30 signees were recruited**, all of whom were from the United States. 18 signed to in-state schools, 7 signed to regional schools, and 5 signed to non-regional out-of-state schools.

The average JGS Class ranking was *573.37*. The player with the lowest JGS Class ranking was an Xavier recruit from Kentucky with a ranking of *206*.

General Statistics:

The following are general statistics and totals I found for my entire study. I decided to keep these general statistics until the end of this article. I believe that it they are misleading if you do not understand the nuances of the group statistics that I explained above.

Average JGS Class ranking of all DI Early Signees: 364.54
Percentage of International Early Signings: 13%
Percentage of In-State Early Signings: 52%
Percentage of Regional Early Signings: 23%
Percentage of Out-of-State Early Signings: 22%

What do we know about the 365th kid in NJGS?

The most important take away about the average student signing to Division One is their scoring differential; most players are .5 or less. This means that they average .5 shots higher than the course rating on an average day. Please note that the course rating is not the Par of the golf course; course rating is approximate amount of shots a scratch golfer should shot. The harder the golf course, the higher the course rating.

The best players have a negative scoring differential. In the 2017 signing class the number one player was Won Jun Lee. His scoring differential was -5. This means that he is beating the average Division One player by approximately 5.5 shots per round and 16.5 shots per tournament. That's a lot!

It is also important to understand that the best players have negative scoring differentials. When you are creating a schedule, you should check the course ratings of the courses. If the course ratings are at par or below, you will need to shoot that score. If they are higher, then a round of 72 or 73 might help.

CONCLUSION

Based on my analysis, the highest average JGS class ranking for any section of the top 300 Division I teams was 573. Therefore, in my opinion a male junior golfer must be in the Top 600 of his recruiting class to be seriously considered by a DI program.

But when everything's said and done, it is important to remember that recruiting is not an exact science. The WAGR and JGS are not the be-all-to-end-all. Other factors such as academics, recruiting in-state, or legacy (having a family member attend a college or university in the past) can influence a coach's decision. My data should only be a **benchmark** for knowing how well you must perform to be a Division I golfer. Hopefully you find this information helpful on your journey to be a collegiate athlete.

LET'S TALK ABOUT MEN'S DIVISION II GOLF...

Division II athletics often get a bad reputation. People assume that Division II sports are considered a much lower level of competition because it is a step down from Division I. Time and again I've seen junior golfers and their parents set their sights on Division I golf teams without even considering the option of Division II. While there is nothing wrong with this, it is important for them to realize that there really is no shame in playing Division II athletics in college.

The Difference Between Division I and Division II Athletics

Division II schools offer a minimum of 10 sports teams (five women and five men) whereas Division I schools offer a minimum of 14 sports teams (seven women and seven men). NCAA rules state that Division I teams can offer 4.5 scholarships while Division II teams are allowed to offer 3.6 scholarships.

What does this mean for Men's Division II Golf Programs?

Ultimately the worth of a team can be demonstrated through the commitment of the administration, donors, and greater community towards the golf program itself. In my opinion, much of this must do with whether a school is "**Fully Funded**" or not. According to the NCAA, a "Fully Funded" team is technically defined by the fact that they can offer the full amount of scholarships permitted. So, while DI teams can offer more scholarships that DII teams, I would estimate that only 50% of DI team's s are considered Fully Funded. Thus, it is very common for Fully Funded DII teams to surpass Semi or Partially Funded DI teams because Fully Funded DII teams have financial access to better resources.

How Well Do Men's DII Programs Stack Up Against Men's DI Programs?

Although drop-off can be significant between Division I and II athletics for sports like football and basketball, this is certainly not the case for men's college golf. Just look at scoring averages between the top 25 teams in both divisions. In the fall of 2016, the top 25 DI men's team saw a scoring average of 71.18. This is impressive to say the least, but what is perhaps more impressive is that **Top 25 Scoring Average for DII men's teams were right on its heels at 72.68**. Moreover, if you compare the average scores of just the top 10 teams in both division, that discrepancy gets even lower: Division I teams average 71.05 while Division II teams average 72.29.

The elevated level of competition at top DII schools is also exemplified at on school-by-school basis. Lynn University, the No. 1 Division II men's golf team, has a fall scoring average of

71.42. This scoring average surpasses DI programs at:

No. 8 Texas A&M
No. 10 Texas
No. 13 North Carolina
No. 20 Oregon

No. 22 Clemson
No. 23 UNLV
No. 25 Georgia Tech

Men's DII No. 2, West Florida University, has a fall scoring average of 71.18, which surpasses the scoring averages at DI schools such as:

No. 8 Texas A&M
No. 9 Oklahoma
No. 10 Texas
No. 11 Georgia
No. 13 North Carolina
No. 18 San Diego State
No. 19 Texas Tech
No. 20 Oregon
No. 21 Duke
No. 22 Clemson
No. 23 UNLV
No. 25 Georgia Tech.

For those of you that still don't believe that DII players can be just as good as DI players, look no further than Golfstat Cup Top 100. The Golfstat Cup Top 100 measures all college players' scoring averages versus par, no matter what their division level. According to this year's Cup, **11 Division II men's golfers rank**

in the Golfstat Top 100, including three in the top 25. The #3 player from Florida Southern University has a scoring average of 69.78, the #15 player from University of Colorado-Colorado Springs has a scoring average of 69.80, and the #25 player from West Florida University has a scoring average of 71.

What About Their Recruits?

In my last blog, I looked at the JGS List of 2016 Early Signees and their JGS rank to illustrate what it takes to be a Division I golfer. I will now examine the list of early signees going to the top 80 Division II schools. I consider these teams to be the most competitive DII programs because they are most likely the ones to be selected to play in the Division II Regional Championships for this year.

Top 25

From a geographic perspective, 24% of recruits were international students and 76% of recruits were from the United States. Out of these players, 24% of them were recruited to out-of-state and 52% of them were recruited in-state. The average JGS 2017 Class Ranking was 510. However, if we take out a University of Northern Alabama (UNA) recruit from Alabama with the outlying ranking of 1938, **the average JGS 2017 Class Ranking is 410**. The lowest ranked player was a West

Florida recruit from Venezuela with a ranking of 84, while the highest ranked player was a UNA recruit from Alabama with a ranking of 723. **Finally, 65% of players were in the top 600 of the JGS.**

Top 26-80

16% of recruits were international students while 84% of recruits were from the United States. Of these players, 50% of were recruited in-state and 34% of players were recruited out-of-state. **The average JGS 2017 Class Ranking was 677.** The player with the lowest JGS ranking was a Grand Valley State recruit from Michigan with a ranking of 168, while the highest ranked player was a Tusculum recruit from Wisconsin ranked at 2062. **60% of recruits were in the top 600 of the JGS.**

There are 215 Division II men's golf teams in the United States, most of which offer 2 spots per recruiting class. This means that **only 430 juniors are recruited to Division II golf teams a year.** If you want to be considered a competitive DII player, it is best to seek out a top 80 school so that you can play in regionals with your team. The average 2017 JGS Class Ranking for early signees at these top 80 schools is 593.5. This means that **you should have to have a JGS of 600 or better to be seriously considered for a top 80 Division II team.**

It should come as no surprise that I gave the same advice to juniors seeking to play DI golf. As I have proven in this article, these top 80 DII programs are just as competitive, if not more competitive, than many DI programs. So, at the end of the day, it is important to put division level aside and simply ask yourself if a school has everything you need from an athletic, academic, social, and financial perspective.

DON'T COUNT DIVISION III OUT JUST YET

Prior to the formation of Division III athletics, the NCAA was split into two divisions. Larger, more funded schools were placed into what is now considered Division I, while smaller schools that wanted less expensive, but still competitive athletic programs were grouped into the "College Division." This division split in 1973, with colleges who wanted to continue giving out athletic scholarships being placed into Division II, and colleges who chose not to offer athletic scholarships being placed into Division III.

The absence of athletic scholarships from DIII schools is what sets it apart the most from DI and DII.

Because of this Division III colleges offer smaller, very limited athletic programs. At these colleges, athletics teams are non-revenue-generating, extracurricular programs that are barred from using endowments or funds whose primary purpose is to benefit the athletes. While this can seem constraining to many, it is not necessarily a reason to discard DIII schools from a junior golfer's search for a college team. DIII programs can still offer a fulfilling athletic experience at a comfortable level of competition for golfers who are looking to play for a team, but wish to direct most of their focus towards academics or other aspects of their college experience.

Just as with Division II men's teams, top Division III men's teams still play at an elevated level. **The average scores of the top 5 and 25 Division III teams are a respectable 72.79 and 74.36**. These scoring averages stay consistently in the 70s until around the 50th best team that has a scoring average of 80.14. For the next 50 or so teams, this number stays relatively consistent, with the 100th best team shooting an average of 80.52. While these numbers certainly aren't anything impressive in the grand scheme of college golf, these players are still performing well above-average for their division, better than some DII programs, and in some cases better than bottom-tier DI programs. Following the 100th best teams, there is a steep drop off the average scores of teams. The 150th best team holds a scoring average of 82.39, while the 200th best team shoots a whopping 88.84.

Even though some teams are far more skilled than others, true competitiveness of DIII golf lies mostly on an individual level. For example, **three Division III players have placed in the Golfstat Cup Top 250**. As I mentioned in my previous article, the Golfstat Cup compares all college players' scoring averages versus par regardless of division level. The #96 player from No. 2 UT Tyler has a scoring average of 71.43, the #139 player from No. 1 Huntington has a scoring average of 71.44, and the #168 player from No. 5 LaGrange holds a scoring average of 71.27. If these players are considered the top collegiate golfers in the country and out-performing DI and DII players alike, DIII golf is clearly nothing to disregard.

If you are interested in being recruited by a top Division III school, feel free to look at who they are recruiting to see how you match up. Once again, I looked at this year's 2017 List of Signees on Golfstat to see how good recruits at the top 25 DIII schools are performing. **The average JGS ranking was 750**. The player with the lowest ranking of 150 is a Claremont-Mudd-Scripps recruit from California, while the player with the highest ranking of 1768 is a Texas-Tyler recruit from Wisconsin. From this data I gather that

a player should have a JGS of about 775 or better to be considered by a top 25 DIII school.

As far as Division III men's golf goes, a player is only going to get out what he puts in. If he wants to take his game seriously and play at an elevated level there is certainly room for him to do so. There is undoubtedly a substantial group of superior golfers to compete against and utilizing practice time and team resources will give him the opportunity to rise to their level. At the same time, if a player is looking to add athletics as a non-serious facet of his college experience Division III gives the player the chance to do so. Whatever the case, I would never discourage a player from playing golf at a collegiate level. It is a unique, enriching experience and an impressive feat regardless of college division.

DIVISION 1 WOMEN'S

I t is only natural, then, that I move to an examination of the early signees on women's collegiate golf teams. Since it is practically every junior girl's dream to play Division I women's golf, I will examine data from the 2016 Division I Early Signees found on the National Junior Golf Scoreboard (NJGS). After comparing this list with the National Junior Golf 2017 Class Ranking and the World Golf Amateur Ranking (WAGR), I hope to draw specific conclusions that will help the average junior girl golfer determine whether or not they have what it takes to play DI golf. Think you have what it takes? Let's look:

Out of the 267 girls that signed early to Division I, Division II, Division III, and NAIA teams, 214 girls signed to Division I teams. The average NJGS class ranking for girls from the United States that signed early to a Division I team was 589. The average WAGR ranking for international junior girl golfers was 1164. Using this data, I found that the 589th girl ranked in the NJGS has an average score of 74.5 and the 1164th ranked girl in the WAGR has an average score of 75.5. So, it is safe to say that a junior girl has a shot at playing Division I golf if she consistently shoots in the mid to low 70s by the time the recruiting process begins in her junior year.

The data collection and conclusions I have drawn may be slightly skewed. Out of the 216 girls, 54 did not have a ranking on neither the NJGS nor the WAGR.

Just because you are not consistently shooting in the mid to low 70s does not necessarily mean that you won't be able to get a spot on a Division I team. There is actually a fairly large discrepancy between top and bottom Division I teams. For example, the top 10% of girls that signed early in 2017 have an average NJGS ranking of 53, meaning that they are consistently shooting 72 at tournaments. (*Please note that I did not include the girls in the WAGR because there were only two international girls in the top 10% and thus was not an adequate amount of data to include in the average*). Thus, if you are looking to play for a top 10% team, your tournament average should be par or better. The bottom 10% of early signees had an average NJGS ranking of 1684 and an average WAGR ranking of 2059. When looking at both rankings, girls typically shoot in the low 80s to high 70s.

While it may seem like this bottom 10% has high scores, it is important to keep in mind that college recruitment is not based on score alone. A girl can still catch the eye of a coach even if they are not shooting their best. One example of this is the fact that many college coaches will want to see where their recruits place in various tournaments. This is because the girl's placement in the tournament demonstrates a level of competitiveness necessary at the college level. It shows that the girl can keep up with her peers. So even if a girl shoots 79 but places in the top 10, it is still worth telling a coach about her performance.

One interesting piece of data I found was that 43% of early signees were recruited to schools that were in the same state, or one to two states away from where they live. Although it is unsure whether there is causation to this correlation, I speculate this could be because coaches like to recruit girls that are used to playing in the same weather conditions that are seen at their college. It makes it easier on players because there does not need to be as much of an adjustment to their college's new course conditions. Because of this, I do not think it would hurt to pay attention to colleges in your geographic location.

Academic performance, connections, character, and personality are also part of the equation. The chances of a junior being recruited to a team can significantly increase if they demonstrate academic prowess, as college teams are always looking to improve their academic standards. If you are aware that you have specific connections through a family member or friend, don't be afraid to use them because a recommendation from a credible source can go a long way. Although connections can be hard to establish if you do not already of them, it is always important to keep in mind that every tournament is an opportunity to network with someone within the golf community. You never know who you will meet and what they can do for you. Finally, college coaches like to know how their future players will act under pressure. Maintaining a calm and cool composure even when things aren't going as planned on the golf course can be very impressive to a coach. Coaches will take note of a player that struggles on one hole but manages to bounce back on the next.

From the outside looking in, there is a perception that female golfers lack the skill and technique male golfers possess. Anyone working within the world of golf knows that this is the farthest thing from the truth. This is particularly evident when looking at the statistics I provided in this post. To further support this point, look at Stanford, the top women's team in the country. This team has a scoring average of 71.6, just .87 strokes less than the men's number one, Vanderbilt. And this level of play amongst female collegiate golfers is only expected to increase, as the number of junior girl's golfers is growing at a rapid pace. According to the PGA of America, the number of junior girl golfers climbed from 4,500-50,000 girls per year from 2010-2015. This means that the number of junior girl's golfers is increasing by at least 9,000 *a year*. From these numbers, it is evident that the level of competitiveness in junior girl's collegiate golf recruitment only continue to expand in the coming years. Thus, a player should always strive to get better and never limit themselves or their potential because someone is always getting better.

WOMEN'S DIVISION 2, 3 AND NAIA

Almost all junior girl golfers aspire to play for a team in college. However, many of these girls only set their eyes on the possibility of playing for a Division I team. While being a Division I collegiate athlete is very impressive, players can often get the same, if not a more rewarding experience playing below the DI level. In my opinion, a junior player should never rule out the possibility of playing for a Division II, Division III, or NAIA (National Association of Intercollegiate Athletes) college team. Even though the average scores may be higher in these divisions, players still get an opportunity to travel the country and play golf at a competitive level. And, as you will see in this blog post, these opportunities are much more abundant than you would think.

Once again, I looked at the list of the 2016 Early Signees found on the National Junior Golf Scoreboard (NJGS). This time, however, I will be examining girls that signed to DII, DIII, and NAIA schools and compare them with the National Junior Golf 2014 Class Ranking as well as the World Amateur Golf Ranking. Using the data that I have collected, here's a bird's eye view on what it takes to be recruited in these three divisions:

In 2016, 267 girls signed early to women's teams, 39 of which signed to Division II schools. 36 of these girls were from the United States and 6 were international players. There were only 3 girls that signed to Division III teams and 11 girls that signed to NAIA teams, all of whom were from the United States. Because the number of girls that signed to DIII and NAIA schools is so small, I decided to average the NJGS rankings of DII, DIII, and NAIA early signees together. The average NJGS Ranking for these girls was 1343, which sets them out to have a scoring average of about 85. The average WAGR for the Division II early signees was 2158, meaning that international players held a scoring average of about 82.2. Therefore, shooting in the mid-to-low 80s by the time a girl begins her recruitment process as a junior will give her a great shot at playing Division II, III, and NAIA golf.

Please note that these scoring and ranking averages are slightly skewed given the fact that 17 of the girls that signed to DII teams and 7 of the girls signed to NAIA teams were not ranked in either the NJGS or the WAGR

Golf is only one half of the student-athlete experience. After all, a player is always a *student* before they are an athlete. DII, III, and NAIA programs take this very seriously. Because there is less of an academic commitment as it relates to schools below the DI level, students have more of an opportunity to focus on their studies. Moreover, while it is of course expected that a player wants to be recruited to a team to follow her passion, a girl can use golf as a vehicle to get a better academic experience. The fact of the matter is that women's DII programs can award 5.4 scholarships and NAIA programs can award 5 grants annually. So, playing for a DII or NAIA school can make it a lot easier on the family finances. While DIII schools are not permitted to award scholarships, many of these schools are superb academic institutions. Mount Holyoke, Williams College, Ithaca College, Washington & Lee, and Washington University in Saint Louis are just a few colleges that offer Division III women's golf. So, if you happen to get contacted by a coach from one of these divisions, it is definitely worth taking a look at a school's academic programs and standings before you before you cast it to the side.

All three of these collegiate divisions offer programs that are easier to play for than DI programs and still offer a superior level of play. Yet even though there are 191 colleges with Division II women's golf teams, 196 Division III women's golf teams, and 138 NAIA women's golf teams, many junior golfers believe that they are "too good" to play below the Division I level. As a result, they will earn a spot on a DI team, but remain on the practice squad for all four years. Although it is indeed nice to say that you play on a DI team, being on the practice squad won't necessarily make you a better golfer if you never actually getting an opportunity to travel.

WHAT'S THE DEAL WITH JUNIOR COLLEGE?

One route many junior golfers leave out in their search for a collegiate golf program is the option of starting out on a two-year junior college team. Although most golfers are eager to jump right into a four-year university, they don't realize that junior college can be a very rewarding experience. Junior college provides students with an opportunity to improve their game as a collegiate athlete while still earning credit towards their college degree. Because of this, junior collegiate golf can be beneficial for players looking to move onto serious NCAA programs. In fact, more and more NCAA golf coaches are looking for transfers from junior colleges that are used to a higher level of play and don't need time to adjust to competing at a collegiate level.

Junior College golf can also be appealing from a financial perspective. **Golf teams in the National Junior College Athletics Association (NJCAA) can give out 8 scholarships a year,** which is the highest number of scholarships offered by any college athletics association in the country. This can be very attractive to families that are looking for the most affordable option for their child's college career, especially because junior colleges have low tuitions to begin with.

There are currently 241 men's and 113 women's golf programs in the NJCAA. Skill level varies widely across the board. Because of this, it is often difficult to judge exactly what it takes to play golf at a junior college. Some teams have very casual programs with players shooting in the high 80s to mid-100s. Such teams are comprised of walk-on athletes who are looking for a nonchalant sport to supplement their college experience. The **top junior college golf teams act as feeder programs for students looking to become serious NCAA athletes**. Since all of my clients are looking for a serious athletic experience in college, I decided to gather statistics on how these top junior college teams are performing.

The Top 5 Men's Junior College Golf programs and their scoring averages are:

Odessa Community College
Individual: **72.8**
Eastern Florida State
Individual: **73.2**
Indian Hills Community College
Individual: **72.44**
Midlands Community College
Individual: **72.69**
Dodge City Community College
Individual: **73.68**

The Top 5 Women's Junior College Golf programs and their scoring averages are:

Daytona State College
Individual: **74.08**
Seminole State
Individual: **75.47**
Tyler Junior College
Individual: **77.85**
McLennan Community College
Individual: **80.21**
Redlands Community College
Individual: **80.13**

Within these teams are some excellent individual players; in men's junior college there are six individual players for the year that are averaging under par. There are another twelve that are averaging better than 73. In women's junior college, there is one player averaging better than par and seven more averaging better than 76.

As someone who coached junior college for 3 years, from my personal experience, a good junior college record can lead to having opportunities at a major conference school. In my time as the Redlands Community College Women's Golf team, we were a dominate force in junior college golf and our best players went on to play at Missouri, Florida, Tennessee and University of Southern California. Over the past couple years, I have seen the best junior college boys go to schools like Colorado and Florida.

It is important to understand that Junior College is a great fit for students who are not passionate about school, need more time to mature or are late developers. At junior college, each of these students will have up to 2 years to gain college credit but also develop their games. I am a stronger believer in the system and would encourage people to seriously consider it as an option.

ELITE ACADEMIC
INSTITUTIONS

Some of the people reading this book will be interested in attending a high end academic school. In this chapter, we will introduce you to some of the data around Ivy League and other elite academic schools.

Academic students need to understand the benchmarks, to allot their time correctly. To be a strong consideration for an elite academic school with golf, academically you will need to have a GPA of around 4.0 with two or more honors classes and an SAT of more than 1400 with at least 700 in each section or corresponding ACT. The quality of the school you attend, as well as your class rank (if available) may also be considered. Location can also play a role in the admissions process. Top tier academic schools will have the most interest from large city centers concreted in the north or north-east corridor, places like Chicago, New York and Philadelphia. Therefore, students from less represented states or locations like Florida, Mississippi or Wyoming may have an advantage in the process.

According to National Junior Golf Scoreboard, in 2017 Yale, Princeton and Brown Women's Golf signed a total of six players. Their NJGS rankings were 137, 32, NR, 81, 29 and NR. The average for the players was 69.75.

One of the signees for University of Pennsylvania was Chelsea Liu. She was not ranked in NJGS but was ranked in the WAGR. Her WAGR ranking was 2388 over five tournaments in 2016, including three AJGA's and the Florida Junior and Amateur stroke play. In her 3 AJGA's her stroke average was 76.22. In all five tournaments, her stroke average was 75.6.

Georgetown and Lehigh Women's Golf also had golf signees listed. Between these programs, they signed another four players. There rankings were 71,103, 140 and 233, with an average of 136.75.

In 2017, Princeton won the Ivy League Championship at Orange Tree in Orlando, Florida with a total of 891 (296-302-293). Please note, Orange

Tree is one of the hardest golf courses in the country, with extremely narrow fairways lined by out of bounds and firm, fast and undulating greens. Georgetown also won the Big East Conference championship with a total of 896 (296-303-297).

For Men's Golf, National Junior Golf Score Board, has six men's signees listed from Columbia and Yale. Their rankings are 225, 351, 117, 349, 236 and 182, with an average of 243.33. Schools like Middlebury and Colgate also had players listed. The Colgate players were ranked 356/989 and the Middlebury player was ranked 980.

The higher rank for these players, could be a result of the success schools like Virginia, Vanderbilt, Duke, Georgia Tech and Stanford have in men's golf. After the 2017 season, Duke was the ACC Team Champion with a score of -14 for 3 days. These schools also had very good national rankings: Vanderbilt #2, Stanford #5, Virginia #18 and Duke #19 and Georgia Tech #21.

In 2017, Harvard won the Men's Ivy League Championship with a total of 874 (293-292-289) at Stanwich Golf Club in Connecticut. Having played the course, I can attest to the fact that it is a strong test of golf at any point and this event was played in late April when the weather was fair at best.

Elite academic schools in men's and women's golf are blessed to have options of players with strong academic and athletic resumes. These students often have close to perfect GPA's and test scores above 1400 (combined, 2 sections), as well as earn athletic rankings better than the average Division 1 player.

ADVICE IN THE SCHOLARSHIP PROCESS

The Four Inputs of the Scholarship Process

It is important that parents and student-athletes understand that coaches look at four main inputs when recruiting — golf, academics, interview and finances.

<u>Golf</u>: The three main components for golf are scoring average, head-to-head record and rounds under par. For boys, it is very important to have some rounds under par. It is also important to note that coaches will strongly consider head to head over score in situations where the field is strong and conditions

are tough. Strong technical golf swings are also very important, as well as a clear passion for golf.

Academics: SAT/ACT, GPA, class rank and high school reputation are the most crucial factors.

Interview: The interview is a critical part of the process and is the biggest reason that students get opportunities, for several reasons. It is important to remember that in Division I golf there are 300 schools. Of these it is likely that only about 10 percent have a chance to win a national championship. This means 90 percent do not. For these coaches, while it is important to compete in their conferences, it is equally as important to have ***really good kids that they like and do not cause problems***! Most coaches do not get paid enough to deal with headaches. If during the interview, they feel a student (or parent) is high maintenance and not going to make a significant contribution to the program, they could pass on the student-athlete.

Finances: To be successful in men's golf, I think coaches need to get three to five players on low scholarships (less than 30 percent) so that they can spend money on super stars, who generally command more than 80 percent.

There are 988 men's golf programs in the United States — Division I, Division II, Division III and NAIA — with 729 on the women's side. The inputs determine how many of them you can attend. For example, if you are a female golfer with a perfect SAT, unlimited budget and a scoring average of 71, you have all 729 options. On the other hand, if you have a 700 SAT, 1.7 GPA, a $5,000 budget, and a 100-scoring average, you may only have two to four options.

The Recruiting Funnel

Let's use the image of a funnel to help explain the recruiting process. At the top of the funnel are some 250 to 500 student-athletes. In the middle are the unofficial visits. This is a tricky number because some schools are open to many visits, especially by local student-athletes or people with ties to the program. This can put the number higher but in general it will be between 15 and 25 unofficial visits per year. Next are the official visits. These will number no higher than six most years. Then at the bottom are the student-athletes who commit and play on the team; normally just two or three, and perhaps just one.

Before the college decision, I want to share the story of Caroline Sacks. Caroline's story has been told in the book, *David and Goliath: Underdogs, Misfits, and the Art of Battling Giants*, also by Malcolm Gladwell. A talented student, Ms. Sacks found herself struggling in her senior year to decide whether to attend Brown University or the University of Maryland. Based on brand and prestige, she chose Brown and quickly found that the competition level was much more then she anticipated. Quickly she was unable to compete and gave up her goal of being a scientist.

For parents guiding a student-athlete, it is important to understand their child's selection of a university from a holistic perspective. Of course, you will be seeking to identify the best school among all those the student could gain admission to. Further, however, you need to weigh such factors as their maturity, their social skills and their survival skills. Under the latter category are such questions as how well they might adapt to campus life and independence, how responsible are they, how hard are they likely to work at school, how high are the academic standards, and how their success at the school will match their prior success. You should also consider what support systems are in place at each school on their list.

In order for this whole process to be successful, it is important for the parent to mentally separate what they want from what is ultimately best for their student. All parents want the best for their children but for each child this is unique. Some students don't love school, but if you are thoughtful, you can put them in an environment where they can compete, earn good grades, have a great experience, mature and perhaps position themselves for graduate work in the future. On the other hand, a parent can push hard for the better school and have their student select it, only to find that, like Caroline, they get uncomfortable, change majors and put aside dreams. I encourage parents to be thoughtful about the decision and avoid defaulting to the best schools out of hubris.

Who Does Well in College Golf

I believe that college golf has a key role in the development of the golfer; it allows them to build experience in tournament competition, as well as work on many of the skills needed to play elite golf. These skills include being independent, competitive, self-motivated and being able to bounce back after a poor tournament.

In many cases, what college golf does not offer, is the ability to continue to build your technical golf swing. Golfers should be encouraged to invest heavily in their junior career to ensure they have a stable and repetitive swing. This will serve them well in their college days. This advice is contrary to what most parents and students hear. Instead, so many within the junior golf community encourage playing a lot of tournaments to gain exposure and earn a scholarship. In my opinion this is only good advice if you have already spent sufficient time building great ball control. The nature of college golf is so competitive, that if you do not have these skills when you arrive, you are not likely to can improve your skills and you may not play as much as you would like.

For junior golfers, late in the process, I would encourage them to think long term about their golf. If you are a junior, you may consider using not only a GAP year but also maybe attending a junior college for a year. This will allow you time to develop the skills necessary to make the best of your time in college.

Special note to guys and girls who love to practice: Make sure in the recruiting process you are very open about this preference. Many coaches like to create "competitive environments" in which they expect players to play a lot (either on the golf course or games in practice). This environment can be very different for someone who loves to practice; they have to be open to making the change. If they are not, then it is likely the result will not be positive.

School Decision

Before the college decision, I want to share the story of Caroline Sacks. Caroline's story has been told in the book, *David and Goliath: Underdogs, Misfits, and the Art of Battling Giants*, also by Malcolm Gladwell. A talented student, Ms. Sacks found herself struggling in her senior year to decide whether to attend Brown University or the University of Maryland. Based on brand and prestige, she chose Brown and quickly found that the competition level was much more then she anticipated. Quickly she was unable to compete and gave up her goal of being a scientist.

For parents guiding a student-athlete, it is important to understand their child's selection of a university from a holistic perspective. Of course, you will be seeking to identify the best school among all those the student could gain admission to. Further, however, you need to weigh such factors as their maturity, their social skills and their survival skills. Under the latter category are such questions as how well they might adapt to campus life and independence, how responsible are they, how hard are they likely to work at school, how high are the academic standards, and how their success at the school will match their prior success. You should also consider what support systems are in place at each school on their list.

For this whole process to be successful, it is important for the parent to mentally separate what they want from what is ultimately best for their student. All parents want the best for their children but for each child this is unique. Some students don't love school, but if you are thoughtful, you can put them in an environment where they can compete, earn good grades, have a wonderful experience, mature and perhaps position themselves for graduate work in the future. On the other hand, a parent can push hard for the better school and have their student select it, only to find that, like Caroline, they get uncomfortable, change majors and put aside dreams. I encourage parents to be thoughtful about the decision and avoid defaulting to the best schools out of hubris.

Parents Role

I would like to speak to the parent's role in the process. For me, their role in guiding their son/daughter depends greatly on their ability to view the process as an important opportunity for their child to grow and develop. In my experience, parents often become too attached to the process from a personal perspective and start having an agenda. For example, parents might want the student to attend a certain school that has a prestigious name but they do not realistically assess whether their student has the academic or athletic requirements to be successful in that environment. The process should be about finding their student a place to succeed; to get a great education, deepen their passion for education, connect with innovative ideas/people and feel confident to be a contributing member of society.

Academics vs. Athletics?

It is important for parents and student-athletes in grade 10 to take a serious look at the academic route versus the athletic route to college. If you want to go to an elite academic school, I recommend a goal of 700 on all sections of the SAT and an average golf score of 75 strokes or lower per 18 holes.

If you are trying to be a great golfer and go to a school that turns out tour players, I would suggest a scoring average from 71.5 to 72.5, top-100 WAGR or better and a combined 900 on your SATs. If you want to be an early commit/signee selection, you must realistically be within the top 100 on the Junior Golf Scoreboard and between 250 and 500 on the WAGR.

The toughest scenario for a high school student-athlete is to be is in the middle, because it is more of a challenge to find a fit. In the middle means, you have scored about a 1010 on the SAT and you are a 75 or higher shooter. You are distinct in neither respect and there are hundreds, if not thousands, of people like you. In this situation, it is best to send emails that lead off with your best quality. This could be a great golf swing or maybe steady improvement in golf scores over the prior two years or even a story about being new to the game. There are some programs that are intrigued by these types of players. The key is to successfully discover them, so don't be afraid to send out a lot of emails!

Once you have chosen between academics and athletics as your path, have that be reflected in the way you set up your communications, whether via email or other methods. If you are trying for entry into a top academic school, put your GPA and test scores very early in the email, perhaps even in the subject line. This is important because although there is great interest in the leading academic schools among top junior golfers, most of these potential applicants do not meet the requirements. By meeting the requirements, you open up the opportunity to be recruited. If your strength is your golf scores, and you're going the athletics path, communicate on that basis. You may want to lead with your ranking (WAGR, NJGS or Golfweek) or scoring average. You probably want to follow this with a swing video and some information about your practice schedule or development plan.

I'm only Coming for Golf
Over the years, I have heard a lot of players, especially international students, who struggle, say that the only reason they want to attend school is because of golf. In fact, almost 20 years ago, I was one of those students. Looking back, I would say that I misunderstood the

amount of experience I would get through the college process. School is an important part of the process, including those dreaded general education classes (my least favorite was music appreciation), however you should gain a lot of other experiences at college. Don't undervalue these experiences as part of your development towards your goals.

The other problem with this thinking, is that during the decision-making process you might tend to hone in on one to three things. For example, for me, Campbell was a wonderful experience because it had 36 holes of golf on campus in nice weather. However, it was not a fit intellectually, spiritually, socially or for the coach. As a result, when golf was going bad, I had no connection to the school and was 100% completely miserable.

The best time to get this experience is during a visit. My advice is to never commit to a school without doing the following:

1. Stay in the dorms and spend time with your team mates
2. Spend time alone with the coach and have a specific talk about what they will do in your personal development
3. Have your personal coach and college golf coach connect

4. Spend time in a class, eat in the cafeteria and see the campus in different weather. For example, if you are from the North and thinking about University of Central Florida, see the campus in August when the temperature is the hottest. Likewise, if you are not accustomed to wintry weather and thinking about a northern school go visit in January or February.

How much do you want to Play?

A major topic of conversation among coaches, players and parents is playing time. Over the years, I have heard a variety of theories on playing time. Opinions have come from students who want to be the best, who want to play on a competitive team where they are in the middle, and everywhere in between.

In my opinion, the best attribute of college golf is the opportunity for you to test your game in competition against top players 24 days per year (maximum number of tournament days by NCAA Division One rules). I would not be afraid to be the best player on the team because that would make me less likely involved in the "qualifying process." This allows you to focus on improving your game and proper practice to prepare for the tournament.

What can you live with?

I have visited over 800 campuses. That experience has taught me that every school has a lot of positive factors. However most of them have at least one, or perhaps two, characteristics that are not ideal. These include everything from location to practice facilities to playing time to coaching to quality of education. It is important that during the visit the student-athlete and family identify the downside of each potential school and then discuss them.

It is extremely likely that after you make your decision, you will feel some level of buyer's remorse. Buyer's remorse is fueled by the feeling that you are missing out on something. *The problem is that no school is perfect, so no matter where you go there will most likely be a downside or two. You should make sure you are aware of these negatives before you make the commitment and that they are things you know you can live with! This is a crucially important point.*

THE SEARCH PROCESS

Where should I be looking?

Locate your ranking on National Junior Golf Scoreboard, then under Rankings and Honors look for the College Signings selection and click on that link. Follow directions to re-display the listings so that instead of being alphabetical it is sorted by Scoreboard Class Ranking. Compare your own ranking with the rankings of those who have signed. Which schools did the 10 people *closest to you in the ranking* sign with?

Also consider –

1. Do they have athletes on the NJGS list that are close to me in ranking?
2. How many student-athletes do they have graduating for my year? What type of players are they?
3. Do I meet the average academic requirements for the school?
4. How much demand is this school likely to have? Remember schools in place like Florida and California not only have high demand, they also have many outstanding local options. (http://golfweek.com/news/2015/mar/12/ncaa-college-golf-players-geography-statistics/)
5. How many student-athletes do they have from my state or country?
6. Do I know anyone on the team?
7. Do I have any connections to the school?

Top programs are always trying to recruit golfer's good enough to play No. 1 on their team. Don't make the mistake, when studying a golf program, of focusing on the scoring average of the players in the No.4 through No. 7 slots. If you want to play major conference golf you need to either be a No. 1 talent or have a strong tie to the school. Strong ties include parents as alumni, in-state residency, personal connections between the college coach and someone close to you and a high school GPA that would rank in the top 10 percent of incoming freshmen at that college.

Communicating with Coaches and Making Visits

The data in this book has provided you an idea on how your National Junior Golf Scoreboard might fit with different schools. Based on this research, I would make a list of 20 schools that have signed players like you last year and in which you are interested.

Formatting Your Resume

Every email should include graduation year, ranking (NJGS or WAGR), and academic and athletic results. I would always suggest formatting your resume in a way that best represents your strengths. For example, if you have a great academic record and wish to attend an elite school, you should start with your test score and GPA. If you are an outstanding athlete with a great swing, you want to start with scoring average and a swing video.

I would guess that the average coach is going to look at your material for between 20-25 seconds. During this brief glance, they will be looking to see why you would be a strong addition to their team. Supporting material should be easily accessible - SAT result, GPA, NJGS ranking, upcoming schedule and swing video. Use a YouTube link for your swing video.

If you have done the research correctly, you should hear back from at least 25 percent of the schools within 24 hours. If you don't hear back from any of the schools within five days, it is probably due to poor research on your part.

Swing Videos

Swing videos are only good if a coach can open it! My best advice is to always upload swings to YouTube and include the links in the emails. Making it more challenging then point and click is likely to result in the whole email being deleted.

It is also important that videos are framed correctly; the person should take up the majority of the space. Videos should be shot from down the line and face on and should include an iron and driver in full speed. I have never cared to watch introductions and do not believe they need to be professionally edited. They can simply be a swing clip, properly framed, shot from a phone camera.

Best Times to Send Emails

Most college tournaments happen Saturday until Tuesday or Wednesday, so the best days to send emails to coaches during the school year are Wednesday and Thursday. The best months to email coaches are November, January, June and July. The worst times are the last week of August and first week of September, most of May and middle of December until the New Year. These are typically times when coaches reserve time for their families.

Number of Emails

I would start with about 20 schools, sending the emails during the times suggested. If you have done this properly then you should expect 2-4 very positive responses within 24 hours. If you do not hear from any schools within 4 days, I would send the emails again. If again you don't hear back then pick schools ranked slightly behind the 20 schools. For example, if the 125 Division One School was on your list and you did not hear back, try emailing the 126-135 Division One School. Continue working down the list until you have 2-4 options with planned visits.

Form Letters

It is important for student-athletes to understand that many coaches use a vast net early in the recruiting process to hedge against missing on late developers. The way they do this is through what is called a form letter. A form letter is a correspondence that describes the college in depth including facilities, success of alumni, recent results, academics, success of school, rankings of academic or athletic, upcoming events and so forth.

Understanding form letters is important. Coaches are going to start with a group of between 100-400 students who receive these letters on a regular basis (between 1-2 times per week for top programs). ***Should you receive one of these, it does not necessarily mean that you are a top recruit and will get an offer. Instead, it means you are in a large group, typically a couple hundred players for one or two spots***

When Coaches respond

When you do hear from coaches, make sure to do the following:

1. Thank them for responding
2. Ask them how they prefer to communicate
3. Ask what additional information they need

Once this is covered, you should be working toward a visit to campus as soon as possible. It bears repeating: A visit to campus is the only want a student-athlete can really understand if that school is a good fit.

When you do make your visit, it is best to have a parent or coach attend with you. It is important that during the visit, they make their own notes based on observations. When you return home, you should sit with whomever accompanied you and compare written notes.

Visiting schools is a major expense. Make sure you understand the difference between Unofficial and Official visits.

Once a coach has responded they may come watch you play, or they may not. Many D2 coaches will not watch you play, instead they will invite you for a campus visit and tryout. A tryout allows them two hours to take you to the course and evaluate your skills. If you are asked to visit and try out, follow these guidelines:

- Make sure to greet the coach and thank them for the opportunity
- Understand that bad shots happen. Make sure if you hit a bad shot then you deal with it maturely. Don't get mad. Play a percentage shot and move forward. Also take the opportunity after the round to admit you hit a bad shot to the coach and let him know how you strategized to save par or bogey on that hole.
- Look the part. Coaches, particularly in the South, are very sensitive to appearance. Wear a belt, have your shirt tucked in, have your shoes cleaned up and be sure your equipment is clean and well-ordered.

- Make sure you are not in the middle of a swing change or have recently taken a lesson. Coaches want players with excellent ball control and are often very leery of players with very technical swings / reliance of coaches.
- If it is an evaluation and you hit a bad shot, politely ask the coach if you may hit another.

The details of a visit

The coach is very likely to provide you a detailed itinerary for the trip. This should include

1. A student host to stay with
2. A tour of the campus
3. Time with academic support people
4. Tour of the golf facilities
5. Meeting most or all members of the current team
6. Meeting the assistant coach
7. Seeing a sporting event on campus
8. Time with coaches (possibly a dinner)

It is very important to use your time alone with the players and coach effectively. This is your chance to ask questions and make sure that the school, golf team and coach are a good fit for you.

Some things you may want to accomplish include:

Interviewing the coach:

What is the coach's philosophy?

What are the coach's strengths and weaknesses?

How does the coach interact with other swing coaches?

How can the coach support you when you turn professional?

How can the coach support you when you go out looking for a job?

Interviewing the other players about their experience:

What other schools did you consider?

What is the best feature of this school? Worst feature?

How do players get to the course?

Has the coach ever cut scholarships?

How does the coach deal with discipline?

How does the coach conduct qualifying? Is it a fair system?

How would you describe the players? *(Note: Coaches generally have a particular type of player in mind. Do you fit with these players?)*

How hard is the school academically? How much support is there?

Understand academics / academic support

Are tutors available?

Is there priority registration for athletes?

How important are academics to the coach?

Dorms

How is the food?

Do students feel comfortable in the dorms?

Who will you live with? Other golfers? Athletes?

How hard is campus to navigate?

Parking, etc.

Play at least one of the golf courses

How do you like it? How does it fit your game? How do your scores compare to average qualifying scores?

How many other courses are local?

If there are limited courses, what condition do you expect the course to be in?

Decision Grid

Before visiting any schools, I would suggest that you take time to set up a decision grid. This grid will have 4 columns. In column one I would list between 3-6 things that are important to you in the decision. These can be things like weather, school, playing time, facilities or coach. In column two you need to rank on a scale of 1-10 how each factor is (1 being low – 10 being extremely important).

Now that you have the decision grid set up, print a copy for yourself and for the person attending the visit with you. At the end of the visit, in column three put the grade you would give the school (again 1-10) on each item.

Now take column 2 and multiply it by column 3 and put the sum in the fourth column under score. Once column four is full, sum the length of the column for a total score.

Spending time and doing this properly will help you immensely in your decision-making process!

Buyer's Remorse
It is very common for a decision that represents a significant commitment to spur anxiety in the decision-maker quite soon afterward. Having chosen which college to attend, many high schoolers experience that sharp pang of doubt and misgiving. If this happens in your case, don't be surprised and don't get into heavy self-criticism. Decisions like this come down to narrow differences and it is human nature to think about other possibilities. Try to be secure in the process.

Thank-You letters.
Throughout this entire process, maybe one of the most important things you can do is taking the time to hand-write and mail a personal thank-you letter to each coach. Trust me; these go a long way!

INSIGHTS INTO HOW COLLEGE COACHES THINK

Rule of the No. 1 player

The No. 1 player rule is something every wise recruiter lives by. The idea is to always be on the recruiting trail in search of someone who can play No. 1 on your team, either immediately or shortly in the future.

The Seven-Year Impact

If a skillful player comes to a college, such as an Oliver Schniederjans at Georgia Tech or a John Rahm at Arizona State, it has roughly a seven-year impact on the program. Not only do these difference-maker players help their teams win, they also help recruit other good players. If as a senior at ASU, John Rahm helps convince a 2016 high school senior, that person will then contribute to the team for another 4 years, making a huge impact on the program.

The Role of Stars in Winning

According to the book by Mark de Rond, "There Is an I in Team," any team with no starting all-star player has less than a one percent chance of winning the NBA championship. By comparison a team with one all-star enjoys a 7.1 percent chance of winning and a 16 percent chance of making it to the finals. He goes on to say, "those with pockets deep enough to field two first-team all-star players have a one-in-four chance of winning a championship and better than a one in three chances of making the finals." He also states that a superstar with a relatively weak supporting cast fares better than a team with five good players.

In college golf, the benchmark for success is the Golfstat Cup. It ranks the top 250 players in both men's and women's golf regardless of division. To de Rond's point, you will find when studying it that here is a strong relationship between the number of top-250 players on a team and the tournament performance of that team.

Passion for Golf

When I left Canada to pursue golf, I was playing maybe 100 days of golf a year. Over night that amount almost tripled. That's a lot more golf and so you want to make sure that golf is something you really want to do. Being honest about this will ensure you have a much better expereince.

Culture

The culture is going to be unique at each school based on a number of different factors such as the size of school, its location and its affiliation with any religious groups. I would encourage families to have a serious talk about their expectations when it comes to these variables.

I am a graduate of Campbell University in central North Carolina. As a middle-class Canadian who attended public high school in Ontario, I was unfamiliar with the culture I discovered at Campbell, a Baptist-affiliated university. It was a surprise to me to see how many students walked around campus carrying Bibles and to notice how deeply religious people were. I was a little shocked and disoriented by it.

One day I saw a sign for a party that was offering free food. There was nothing else on the sign except an address and "BYOB." I hurried out, bought a 24-pack of beer and drove to the address on the sign. When I walked in, I felt all eyes on me and my suitcase of beer. I hadn't known that BYOB at Campbell meant "bring your own bible."

The Law of Attraction

As a coach, I was always interested to see who became friendly with whom during the visit, and during the first couple weeks of school. Over a decade of coaching, I noticed that talented players tend to attract each other, and that problem students tend to flock together, as well.

For the student-athlete it is very important to assess who at the school is likely to make up their "golf team social group." Remember that it is highly unlikely for freshman (or underclassmen) to hang out with seniors; therefore, your group is probably the current freshman. During the visit, it is important to assess their goals and personality as it relates to the student athlete. The closer the match you have in those areas, the better.

Early Playing Dilemma

Playing time is a crucial factor in the decision. With, families and students need to understand that early playing time may be a curse. When the student-athlete is playing golf the first couple weeks of a semester, other students are forming social groups. When the season is finally over and the student has time to socialize, he realizes that many of his classmates have formed groups and are already bonded. Some of these groups will resist new members and often the student-athlete can feel very isolated.

Qualifying

Qualifying for the chance to be one of the official competitors representing your college team in the upcoming tournament is often at the heart of many problems on a team. It should be carefully discussed during the recruiting process. It is critical that the student-athlete understand the basic system of the coach.

Qualifying has many upsides and downside. It encourages competitiveness and rewards players who can shoot good scores on command. However, it also rewards players who might play their "home" or qualifying course well. It also gives a major advantage to upperclassmen who have a lot of experience playing that course (for this reason don't be surprised if you are an upperclassman who ties a freshman in qualifying only to see your coach select the younger player).

I believe the best coaches are going to change qualifying each year based on their squad and variables like the number of skillful players, experience of the players, tournament schedule (times and gaps) and other duties of the coach (family / personal or administrative). For example, if you have two returning All-Americans on your team, your coach would most likely set up a system where three spots are available for the other members of the team to try for. This allows them to include their All-Americans in the lineup every time.

College golf puts a major premium on playing rather than practicing. Golfers face 24 days of competition on the road (8-12 tournaments) and probably another 4-5 qualifying tournaments within seven months (September – November and February to May). That's 12-17 tournaments in just over half a year. This means that players must show up with the proper fundamental skills, including ball control and ideas on how to practice, to be successful.

One year I decided to use the "point system" for qualifying. The system was simple, as I told the members of my team: "If I point to you, you are going to the tournament."

Team Dynamics in Recruiting
Team Dynamics is an interesting part of the recruiting process. From my experience, it is very important

to remember that each year the team is going to be a little different. It is also important to consider the size of the team and the strength of the team and how they interact. Often coaches with smaller teams are going to care a lot more about team chemistry and strongly consider how the players will interact. This may also be a greater consideration among women's coaches and players.

On the best teams in the country, maybe top the 25-30, I think that team chemistry is far less of an issue for coaches. In fact, I have had many experiences in which some of the best teams (and players) don't care at all about their team mates, coaches or chemistry at all! The point is that you should assess the dynamics of the teams you visit and decide if they will be a good fit for your personality and style.

Considerations for the Potential Walk-On
Many players have dreams of playing at major conference schools. With demand, coaches sometimes can get very competitive players on lower scholarships that range from 1-30%. The player must carefully weigh the options and factors like playing time, facilities, school experience and finances.

What to Expect as a Walk-On
Here are some things to expect as a walk on –

1. Better players with more experience getting more playing time. Scholarships are usually award to players with the best record over extended periods of time. Just because you may beat this player by a couple shots in qualifying does not always mean you will play.

2. Seniors are a lot physically stronger then freshman (most of the time)

3. Upperclassmen have a significant advantage in knowing the "home" course

4. Having a strong relationship with the coach is important. If you are going to walk on, make it a priority to go to the coach's office often and spend time with them

Should you get help in the process?

The Binmore Continuum (created by Richard Thaler of the University of Chicago) is the idea that we do trivial things often enough to learn how to get them right, but when we get to larger things, such as buying a home, setting up a mortgage, or getting a job, we don't have much practice at those activities or much opportunity to learn about them, and thus we may not do them so well. This theory also applies to the college scholarship process and why you might want to consider getting assistance in making the right choice. It is the reason that I have developed a business focused on helping families like you connect with schools that meet your athletic, academic, social and financial needs.

At Golf Placement Services, we are specialists in solving your problems and providing the best information. To date we have visited over 800 campuses in 45 states. We have also sent players to 244 different schools in 41 states with a 100% success and a less than 1% transfer rate.

Should you feel like after reading this book, you would like more help, please feel free to reach out to us. We can be reached via email at brendan@golf-placementservices.com.

59490866R00046

Made in the USA
Columbia, SC
05 June 2019